W9-BLX-682

The Salish

CHRISTINE WEBSTER

Weigl

CALGARY

www.weigl.com

Published by Weigl Educational Publishers Limited
6325 10 Street SE
Calgary, Alberta, Canada
T2H 2Z9

Website: www.weigl.com

Library and Archives Canada Cataloguing in Publication Data

Webster, Christine
    Salish / Christine Webster.

(Canadian Aboriginal art and culture)
Includes index.
ISBN 978-1-55388-333-3 (bound)
ISBN 978-1-55388-334-0 (pbk.)

    1. Salish Indians--Juvenile literature. I. Title. II. Series.
E99.S2W43 2007   j971.004'979435   C2007-902193-X

                        Printed in Canada
                1 2 3 4 5 6 7 8 9 0 11 10 09 08 07

Project Coordinator Heather Kissock   **Design** Janine Vangool   **Validator** Keith Thor Carlson, University of Saskatchewan

Photograph credits

Every reasonable effort has been made to trace ownership and obtain permission to reprint copyright material. The publishers would be pleased to have any errors or omissions brought to their attention so that they may be corrected in subsequent printings.

Cover (main): © Canadian Museum of Civilization (VII-G-6, S82-268); **Cover (top left):** © Canadian Museum of Civilization (II-E-18, S95-05958); **Cover (top middle):** CP Images; **British Columbia Archives:** page 8 (E-06423); **Canadian Heritage Gallery (courtesy of Library and Archives Canada):** pages 15 (C-65097), and 16 (C-74694); © **Canadian Museum of Civilization:** pages 6 (T2004-003), 11 left (II-C-352, S94-36801), 14 bottom (VII-D-115, D2002-004800), 18 (VII-D-41 a-b, D2004-07159), 20 (VII-D-158, D2004-07196), 24 left (VII-G-6, S82-268), 29 (VII-G-792, S2001-1049), 30 (II-E-18, S95-05958); © **Canadian Museum of Civilization, James Teit:** page 23 left (1913, 23591); **CP Images:** pages 1 and 21.

We acknowledge the financial support of the Government of Canada through the Book Publishing Industry Development Program (BPIDP) for our publishing activities.

Please note

All of the Internet URLs given in the book were valid at the time of publication. However, due to the dynamic nature of the Internet, some addresses may have changed, or sites may have ceased to exist since publication. While the author and publisher regret any inconvenience this may cause readers, no responsibility for any such changes can be accepted by either the author or the publisher.

CONTENTS

The People

The Salish are a **First Nations** group that live in the southern part of British Columbia, including Vancouver Island. They are also found in parts of the northwestern United States. Canada's Salish are made up of two main groups. The Coast Salish live along the southern coast of the province. They include the Bella Coola, Squamish, Halkomelem, and Straights Salish. The Interior Salish live farther inland. They consist of the Lillooet, Shuswap, Okanagan, and Thompson Salish.

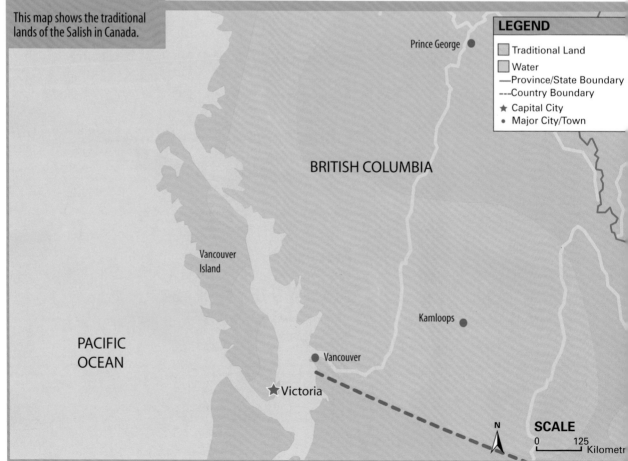

Salish Map

This map shows the traditional lands of the Salish in Canada.

LEGEND
- ☐ Traditional Land
- ☐ Water
- — Province/State Boundary
- --- Country Boundary
- ★ Capital City
- ● Major City/Town

Prince George ●

BRITISH COLUMBIA

Vancouver Island

Kamloops ●

PACIFIC OCEAN

● Vancouver

★ Victoria

N

SCALE

0   125
⊢——————⊣ Kilometr

In the past, the Salish relied on the region's rich land and excellent water sources for survival. The land provided them with plenty of fish, game, berries, and plants. The thick forests provided wood for building houses, sculptures, canoes, and **totem poles**. Villages were built along the coast and on river banks.

The Salish lived independently until the 1790s. This is when Europeans first visited the area. With the Europeans came change. Many of the **traditional** ways of the Salish were challenged by the European lifestyle. Some Salish died of foreign diseases, while others moved to **reserves**. Today, most Salish still live on reserves, but quite a few have also moved into cities and towns.

Today, the Salish live in cities and towns as well as reserves. They often get together in cultural centers to continue learning about their traditional **culture**. They are also passing their traditions on to younger generations. Some Salish schools teach traditional values and customs to the children. Traditional art and languages are also being revived. The Salish continue to hold ceremonies and celebrations traditional of the original Salish Peoples.

The area around Mystic Beach, on the southern tip of Vancouver Island, was once home to a thriving Coast Salish community.

Salish Homes

In the past, the Salish lived in large homes called longhouses. These were one-room homes that housed the entire family, including the father, mother, and children, as well as grandparents, uncles, aunts, and cousins. Longhouses averaged between 12 and 18 metres in length. Wealthy Salish built larger longhouses. Sometimes, they were more than 36 metres long and 6 metres high. The larger homes had walls inside to separate families.

Building a longhouse was a difficult task. It took the efforts of an entire village. The logs used for beams weighed several tonnes. The Salish had to lift them with only small handmade tools and human strength.

Like many West Coast Aboriginal homes, the symbols that adorned a Salish family's home indicated that houses were considered living representations of a family's history.

MAKING OF A HOME

Longhouses were typically made with red cedar planks. This type of cedar was easily split into long and even planks. The floors of the longhouse were made of earth. The inside walls were lined with low platforms or benches. These were for sleeping. Above the sleeping platforms were storage shelves. These held tools, baskets, and clothing. Food and roots hung from the ceiling to dry. Firewood was stored underneath the beds. Mattresses were made from woven mats and animal skins.

The Salish used cedar to build their homes because it was easy to work with and it was more waterproof than other types of wood in the area.

Each longhouse had a number of fire pits inside. The fire pits were located centrally in the house. They were used for warmth and cooking. Smoke holes were found in the ceiling above each fire pit. Slats on the roof could be adjusted to let out smoke or let in light.

Salish Communities

Strong family ties have long played an important role in Salish communities. Each Salish family has certain rights within its community. Fishing sites, the use of specific names, and the right to participate in certain dances and ceremonies can all be determined by family connections. Salish communities remain linked to other villages by marriage. In the past, high-ranking men often had more than one wife. These wives usually lived in their husband's village. This linked villages together by creating an extended family. The extended family was an important part of Salish society.

Like many other communities, a Salish community was shaped by **social status**. In the past, the villages were divided into upper and lower classes. Status was based on many different things. These included **ancestors**, knowledge, religious power, and possessions. It was the family leader's responsibility to make sure all group members were provided for.

In the past, Coast Salish communities were all relate to each other through various family ties. All famil and communities belonged to a common nation.

All Salish people had specific roles expected of them. The men were responsible for hunting and gathering the food. They also carved wood and made tools and canoes. Women tended to the food preparation, made clothing, and cared for the children. They also wove baskets. **Elders** in the village were respected members of the community. They gave advice, helped raise the children, and told stories.

The Salish lived by their own rules for thousands of years. As the European influence became more pronounced, however, this changed. In 1876, the Indian Act was passed. This gave the Canadian government control over First Nations peoples. Many First Nations peoples were moved to reserves. Their children were sent to **residential schools**. Traditional Salish culture was in danger of disappearing. In 1973, Canada's First Nations gained back the right to school their children. Today, First Nations groups have many of their own laws. They are able to develop, conserve, protect, and manage their own lands.

Family connections remain an important part of Salish life.

Salish Clothing

In the past, everything the Salish wore came from the land. The cloth used for clothing was made from bark. The Salish could turn bark into fine threads like fabric. The thread was then woven into soft warm cloths.

To make cloth, a long strip of cedar bark was pulled from the tree. Once removed, the inner layer of bark was separated from the outer layer. Depending on the type of cedar used, the inner bark was then either dried or soaked in water. The Salish used a beater made of bone or hard wood to beat the bark over a sharp board or rock. As the bark was beat, it was bent over the board in small sections. This process shredded the bark into soft threads. Then, it could be woven into fabric. Women wove the cloth into aprons, dresses, cloaks, and skirts.

The Salish still wear their traditional shredded cedar bark clothing at special events.

The Coast Salish wore little clothing in warm weather. Women often wore aprons. Men sometimes wore breechcloths—small flaps of fabric like underwear. Breechcloths were made from animal skins or woven grasses. In colder weather, women wore dresses and cloaks. Salish men dressed in animal skins or cedar shirts and leggings to ward off the cold.

During rainy days, the Salish brought out their cedar ponchos. These were made from strips of bark that were not shredded. The ponchos were uncomfortable to wear but were effective in keeping the rain off. Men wore cedar bark robes for ceremonial occasions or as a coat.

Salish clothing was often decorated with fur, porcupine quills, animal teeth, shells, or bear claws. Necklaces made of bear claws, shells, and beaver teeth were used as jewellery to symbolize wealth.

The Salish used the furs from small animals, such as beavers, rabbits, and squirrels, to make capes and other coverings.

Mountain goat wool was highly valued as a trade item.

The Coast Salish made blankets and shawls from wool. The wool came from mountain goats or from wool dogs. A wool dog is a small dog with long, fine, and soft hair. The Salish treated these dogs much like sheep. When a dog had grown a substantial amount of wool, the Salish sheared the wool from its body with a sharp knife. Then, the wool was cleaned, put on a mat, and pounded with a stick. White clay was mixed with the wool. This made the wool whiter and cleaned it. The bleached wool was then ready to be spun into threads.

Salish Food

Due to the West Coast's rich natural resources, the Coast Salish had an abundance of food. The oceans and rivers provided them with fish, especially salmon. The Coast Salish also had access to many types of shellfish, including butter clams, horse clams, oysters, mussels, and cockles. Whale was also a common food among the Coast Salish. Men were responsible for fishing. They would catch the fish and bring it back to the village. Women were responsible for gathering shellfish.

The land provided the Salish with vegetable sprouts, edible roots, bulbs, berries, and nuts. Soapberries were a popular treat, often used to make sweets such as ice cream and beverages. Deer, bear, elk, and ducks were also hunted for food.

The women were responsible for preparing the food. Salish women cooked using wooden boxes or baskets. The food was put inside the box, along with water and hot rocks. This combination heated and steamed the food. When fish were caught, a small amount would be eaten immediately, while the rest was cleaned and hung in the sunlight or a **smokehouse** to dry. Drying the fish would preserve it for the entire winter.

Black bears are found throughout traditional Salish territory.

Soapberry Ice Cream

Ingredients

250 millilitres of soapberries
63 millilitres of water
sugar

Equipment

Bowl
Spoon or potato masher

1. Place the berries into a bowl.

2. Add 63 mL of water to the berries.

3. Add a dash of sugar on top for sweetness.

4. Mash the berries, water, and sugar together until it foams into a salmon-coloured froth.

5. Enjoy your soapberry ice cream.

Soapberries ripen in mid-summer. This is when they are ready to be picked and used to make ice cream.

Salish Tools

Before European contact, the Salish did not use many metals. They constructed their tools out of rocks instead. Rocks were used for hammers, seed grinders, and weights for fishing nets. Drills were made from sharp stones attached to thin sticks.

Carving tools, such as adzes or wedges, were also made from rocks, and sometimes animal bones. Carving knives were made from sharpened seashells and slate. Wet sand or sandstone rock was used like sandpaper to smooth the blades. The blades were then tied to hardwood handles with bark twine.

Hard stones, such as obsidian and basalt, were used for weaponry. These stones could be flaked into points to make arrowheads or spearheads. They were also used for cutting tools.

Digging sticks were made from hard wood. They were sharpened to a point, and then a horn or antler was added. These sticks were used to dig up earth when planting seeds and bulbs.

Digging sticks could be used to dig up clams and roots.

HUNTING AND TRAVELLING

The Salish made all their own tools for hunting. They caught fish by harpooning, using spears and nets, or by using fishing traps called weirs. A weir is a fencelike structure that is built across a stream or river. It blocks the fish from moving farther up or down river. The fish become crowded inside the weir, making it easy for the Salish to spear large numbers at a time.

The Salish used weirs to catch salmon during their migration. When building a weir, the Salish would permanently drive the posts into the ground, but the fencing was removed when the salmon migration finished. The fencing would be replaced the next year when the salmon came back.

Waters, such as rivers, lakes, and the ocean, provided the main source of food for the Coast Salish. They were also an important means of moving to and from different places. The Salish needed canoes to fish at sea. They used canoes to visit other villages for celebrations.

Prior to European contact, the Salish did not have metal tools to cut down trees. Instead, they developed a unique way of bringing down a tree. They started by lighting a small fire at the tree's base. Feeding the fire with cedar bark chips hollowed the tree trunk until it burned right through and fell. Then, the log was slowly shaped into a canoe using hot water and an adze. Pieces of wood were placed across the middle of the canoe to widen it. Finally, the canoe was sandpapered with dogfish skin and greased with whale oil. Salish canoes could be up to 18 metres long and carry more than 40 people.

Salish Religion

Spirit power remains an important part of Coast Salish life. The Salish feel that spirits can be contacted through dreams and **visions**. The Salish keep these encounters private. Privacy protects the relationship between the spirit power and the person. **Shamans** are very spiritual people. They are believed to have special powers that can scare away evil spirits and cure illnesses. A shaman can also communicate with spirits.

Like many First Nations, the Coast Salish believe all living things, including animals, trees, and humans, have a spirit. Everything is a shell containing a home for the spirit. The Salish have great respect for all living things because of this.

Some Salish practised a type of funeral called a "tree burial." When a person died, he or she was placed in a box. The box was then placed up in the branches of a tree.

The Creator is considered the supreme being. He created everything on Earth. The Salish always give thanks to the Creator for their good fortune. Giving thanks is a form of respect. The Creator is also looked to for guidance.

The Salish hold a variety of religious ceremonies. They use dancing, **oratory**, and music in these ceremonies. Today, as in the past, Coast Salish people turn to certain animals as spirit helpers. These can range from salmon to wolves to mosquitoes. The spirit helper is considered a guide who will assist the person in his or her activities.

The Coast Salish believe that the wasp and mosquito are among the strongest **supernatural** entities. Since the wasp and mosquito are fierce fighters that repeatedly attack much larger animals, they were the preferred spirit helper of people who wanted to be warriors. The mosquito is also considered an ideal spirit helper for certain types of shamans. This is because the mosquito is known to suck blood from people it lands on and shamans are required to suck or pull evil spirits from people who are sick.

The wolf is considered to be the protector of sacred places.

Ceremonies and Celebrations

The Salish marked special occasions with celebrations such as the potlatch. Potlatches provided wealthy people with the opportunity to mark important life events, including the birth or marriage of a child. Guests were invited to share food and receive gifts or payment from the host. Potlatches could include local village members and elite members from other villages as well. Guests were seated by social status, with the highest ranking member served first.

The goal of the potlatch was to share news and demonstrate the wealth and generosity of the host. More food than necessary was always served, and leftovers were sent home with guests. This was so the guests would spread the word about the hosts' generosity. Gifts were also given out. These included important items such as carved cedar boxes, canoes, and **coppers**.

Cedar boxes were useful gifts. They served as household furniture and food containers and were also used as storage bins.

Some hosts put themselves into bankruptcy trying to outdo others at potlatches. Some even destroyed their own property to show their wealth. The more things destroyed, the wealthier the person must be, since they could afford to replace items. Sometimes, these events were used to pay debts. The guests would then be witnesses to a paid debt from one person to another.

Potlatches continue to play an important role in Salish culture. Today, the events are held to celebrate baby showers, birthdays, graduations, and anniversaries. Gifts given out include dishes, artwork, blankets, and money. Potlatches today can last between 12 and 24 hours.

Salmon remain an important food source for the Salish. They have developed many ways to ensure the salmon's well-being, including the "first salmon" ceremony. This ceremony is designed to ensure that the salmon always return to the waters near Salish villages on their way to the **spawning** grounds.

Each spring, when the first salmon is caught, it is brought back to the village, where it is welcomed with a ceremony that includes drumming and singing. The salmon is opened so that its spirit can be released. It is then cooked and shared by all the villagers. The bones and other remains are returned to the water amid more drumming and singing. By showing this respect, the Salish believe that the spirit of the first salmon will return to its underwater home and encourage other salmon to come to their village.

A Salish legend describes the salmon as the chief of all the fish that the Salish use for food.

Music and Dance

Salish **rituals** often include music and dancing. Drumming is an important part of Salish music. Salish drum frames are made from wood. On the top is a piece of stretched animal hide. Sometimes, elaborate paintings cover the drum. The drum is used for many things. People listen to it, dance to it, tell stories with it, and sing along with it.

Singing remains a big part of the Salish life. In the past, it was even more so. When two people married, the family of the groom would arrive at the bride's village singing songs from their ancestors. After the wedding, the bride would be put in the groom's canoe to be taken back to his village. They would leave the site of the wedding singing again.

The Salish used both handheld drums and box drums. Box drums were typically made from cedar.

CEREMONIAL DANCING

Many rituals continue to take place in the winter after a long season of fishing. As in the past, people crowd into longhouses to participate in a winter dance called *seyewen*. Dancers have elaborate costumes, each part holding special significance.

Not everyone can become a winter dancer. Winter dancers have to be dedicated to their **spiritual** beliefs. Once becoming a dancer, they have to leave their old life behind and accept the guidance of a spiritual leader. New dancers spend a few weeks secluded in a tent of blankets inside the longhouse. This time allows them to connect with their spirit helper. During the day, the dancers walk in the woods and take baths in cold streams. They also spend time learning from their elders. The elders teach them the songs and dances they perform at seyewen.

The Salish believe that all of their music and dancing comes directly from Earth.

Language and Storytelling

There are about 23 different languages spoken among the various Salish groups. These languages all belong to a family of languages called Salishan. Each language group has its own unique language elements. These are called dialects and are a result of different word pronunciations. The Salishan language consists mostly of consonant clusters. For example, one word might have 13 consonants in a row with no vowels in between.

Unfortunately, Salishan languages are **endangered**. Some of the 23 Salishan languages have fewer than 12 fluent speakers. Most of these people are between 60 and 80 years of age. Steps are now being taken to teach these languages to younger generations of Salish. Teaching will protect not only the language, but Salish history and culture as well.

Today, many organizations have been formed to teach children how to speak the Salishan language and preserve it for future generations.

Protecting Salishan languages from being lost will also help keep Salish stories in existence. Storytelling was a traditional form of entertainment for the Salish. They recounted their hunting adventures and the activities of supernatural ancestors. Stories also allowed the Salish to pass on wisdom and to teach lessons to others. Elders often told stories and legends to younger Salish to provide them with direction.

The frog is an important creature in Salish stories. The frog is an honoured creature. It is the keeper of sacred seasons. The Salish believe that the frog announces the beginning of each new year by singing. The singing signals the onset of a new cycle. It reminds the Salish to put aside winter things, such as winter dancing and potlatches, in favour of new activities. The frog can be found in many Salish stories, art, and carvings.

Storytelling taught Salish children about morals, beliefs, and traditions.

Salish Art

The Salish are known for their excellent craftsmanship in carving. They were especially known for the large totem poles they carved from enormous cedar logs. The totem poles usually took the form of humans, birds, or other animals. Sometimes, they were used to represent ancestors or spirit helpers. Totem poles are also carved to mark important events, such as potlatches.

The Salish were known for their engravings. Engravings were etched onto everyday items, including spindle whorls. Spindle whorls were used to help spin wool.

CEDAR BASKETS

Totem poles are important because they pass on Salish traditions and honour sacred spirits.

Coast Salish women were known for their skill in making woven cedar baskets. They used the bark and the roots of cedar trees to create the baskets. Roots were gathered near a water source so that they were more pliable. It could take a long time to follow the course of the roots as they were sometimes up to 10 metres long. Cedar bark was stripped from tree trunks in such a way that it did not harm the tree.

Baskets could be decorated in a variety of ways. Often, strips of bitter cherry bark were woven in with the cedar root. The bark was naturally red. Sometimes, it was dyed black.

Hand-carved serving trays, bowls, and even wooden ladles were carved in an artistic way. Some items were even engraved, with designs and patterns carved into the wood. Bowls were carved out of a type of wood called alder. After the shape was carved, fish oil was rubbed over it to give it a polished sheen. Handcrafted objects were often given as gifts. Sometimes, they were traded to Europeans for other goods.

Today, the Salish continue to carry on these artistic traditions. They carve and engrave wood and other items. They do this by studying the work of their ancestors in detail to bring the past forward.

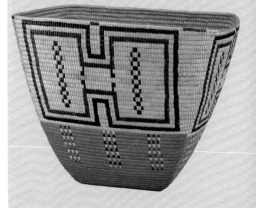

The 13 Moon System

The Salish created a system for measuring time that focussed on cycles and the natural flow of life. The system was called the 13 Moon System because it was based on the cycles of the moons. Each moon in the cycle was accompanied by specific **economic** and cultural activities. The appearance of the elder moon in January signified the most important ceremonial time of year. The elder moon was a time for building character, sharing family gatherings, and restoring relationships. It was at this time that the elders taught young people work skills.

The 13 Moon System was used to indicate when certain resources should be harvested.

Today, many Salish communities feel that European influences have caused them to lose their connection to the 13 moons. This loss threatens Salish culture and spiritual beliefs. Many elders are trying to bring the 13 Moon System back to the younger generations. Schools on reserves have incorporated it into their education programs.

MODERN ARTIST

Susan Point

Susan Point is a Coast Salish artist who lives on the Musqueam First Nation Reserve in Vancouver, British Columbia. She uses traditional Salish artistry to create her art.

Susan began her career in art by engraving Coast Salish designs onto bracelets, pendants, and earrings. She then became interested in the Coast Salish use of the spindle whorl. Spindle whorls were intricately carved with beautiful animal or human designs. Susan used these designs to create silk-screen prints.

As Susan developed her skills, she began to experiment more. She turned to other art forms. By the 1990s, Susan was using her knowledge of Coast Salish art to create three-dimensional sculptures out of wood, polymer, clay, and glass.

Susan has garnered much attention because of her art. She has been hired to create pieces throughout British Columbia. Susan was chosen to make a piece of art as a gift from the Government of Canada. It was created to commemorate the opening of the National Museum of the American Indian at the Smithsonian Institute in Washington, DC.

Susan's art can be found worldwide. Architects and developers place Susan's art in their buildings. Susan has won the National Aboriginal Achievement Award for her work as a Salish artist.

A sculpture Susan created greets visitors at the Vancouver International Airport.

Studying the Past

Archaeologists help us to learn about past cultures. They dig up items left behind from ancestors of the Salish. By studying these findings, they learn more about where the Salish lived, how they lived, and the activities they did in the past.

The earliest Salish ancestors are believed to have lived in British Columbia at least 9,000 years ago. Archaeologists have many findings to support this theory. They have found basic tools made from bones. They have also found anchors made of rocks. Mounds of buried shells have been found, telling us that early Salish ate a great deal of shellfish. All these items help put together pieces of the Salish way of life that may otherwise be forgotten.

By studying British Columbia's waters, archaeologists know that Salish watercrafts had to be strong enough to withstand rough currents.

TIMELINE

7,000 BC
Archaeological evidence indicates **indigenous** peoples were living in British Columbia.

Pre-European Contact
The Salish hunt animals, gather berries, and catch fish. They build settlements along riverbanks and the ocean coast.

1778 AD
The first European contact with the Salish is made by Captain James Cook on the west coast of Vancouver Island.

Early 1800s
The Coast Salish begin trading fur with Europeans. In return, they receive blankets, decorations, copper pots, guns, and ammunition. Contact with Europeans and trading increases quickly.

1858
The British Columbia government begins creating reserves for the Coast Salish.

1876
The Indian Act is passed by Canadian Government. This limits the control First Nations peoples have over their lives.

1880s
Cultural and religious ceremonies, such as the potlatch and winter dance, are outlawed. The Salish are refused the right to school their children.

1973
The First Nations begin taking steps to school their children on their own.

1996
An agreement is signed giving First Nations the right to pass their own laws, as well as to develop, conserve, protect, and manage their own lands.

The Europeans brought the skill of knitting to the Coast Salish, who used it to create the Cowichan sweater. These sweaters are known for their warmth and unique designs.

Weave a Basket

The Salish were known for their sturdy baskets. They used materials such as cedar root and cherry bark to weave beautiful but useful containers. Other materials can be used to weave baskets as well. Use these instructions to make your own basket out of paper.

Materials	construction paper	pencil
	scissors	tape or glue
	ruler	

1. Cut the construction paper into 18 strips. They should be 2.5 centimetres wide and 43 centimetres long. Lay five of the strips parallel to each other.

2. Take another strip of paper, and weave it over and under the five strips. Try to keep the strips close together to make the weave tight.

3. Continue weaving strips until five are woven through, creating a square in a checkerboard pattern.

4. Fold the strips up on all four sides to form the sides of the basket. Use the ruler to make a sharp crease.

5. Glue two strips together to make a long strip. Weave this strip into the sides of the basket. Fold and glue the strip at each corner of the basket to make a square shape. When the first row is complete, cut off any remaining paper, and glue the ends together at the corner. Then, weave the remaining strips in the same way to create your basket.

6. To finish the basket, glue all of the strips to the top row, and trim what remains to make an even edge on all four sides.

Further Reading

Discover the beauty of Salish art by looking at *Contemporary Coast Salish Art* by editors Rebecca Blanchard and Nancy Davenport (University of Washington Press, 2005).

Find out more about the Coast Salish by reading *Northwest Coastal Region: Coast Salish Peoples* (Native Americans of North America) by Mary Null Boule (Merryant Publishers, 2000).

Websites

Learn more about the Interior Salish at
**www.livinglandscapes.bc.ca/
thomp-ok/ethnic-agri/first.html**.

Explore a Coast Salish house at
**www.civilization.ca/aborig/
grand/ghhe6eng.html**.

See more of Susan Point's artwork at
www.susanpoint.com/home.html.

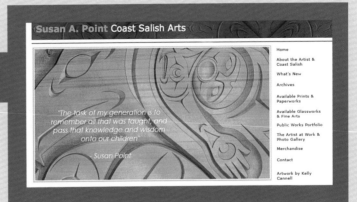

GLOSSARY

INDEX

ancestors: relatives who lived a very long time ago

archaeologists: scientists who study objects from the past to learn about people who lived long ago

coppers: engraved metal slabs that were used as symbols of wealth and prestige

culture: the arts, beliefs, habits, and institutions considered as being characteristic of a specific community, people, or nation

economic: having to do with the management of income and expenses

elders: the older and more influential people of a group or community

endangered: in danger of disappearing

First Nations: members of Canada's Aboriginal community who are not Inuit or Métis

indigenous: living naturally in a certain area or environment

oratory: the art of public speaking

reserves: areas of land set aside for First Nations peoples

residential schools: boarding schools for Aboriginal children set up by the federal government

rituals: systems or forms of ceremonies

shamans: religious people who were believed to have special powers

smokehouse: a building where fish is treated with smoke to preserve it

social status: a person's ranking within a community

spawning: the time when salmon lay their eggs

spirit power: a non-human being that is able to perform acts that humans cannot

spiritual: sacred or religious

supernatural: having to do with forces outside the known laws of nature

totem poles: large, upright poles that are carved and painted with First Nations emblems

traditional: having to do with established beliefs or practices

visions: messages received while in a dreamlike state